SHINING YOUR ARMOUR

FOR MARRIED MEN ONLY

The Lost Art of Romance
by Gabriel H. Vaughn

Oil Painting and Drawings by Wayne Hovis

Cartoons by Dee DeLoy

Shining Your Armour Publishing
1018 West Harvard Street, Orlando, FL 32804

SHINING YOUR ARMOUR: THE LOST ART OF ROMANCE

Gabriel H. Vaughn

Copyright © 1990 Printed in the United States of America
ISBN: 0-9628733-0-6

I dedicate this book to God, the Father.
Because of the example of His Son
we can know how to show love
to one another.

Table of Contents

INTRODUCTION

A great realization is sweeping America today. Satisfaction in personal relationships doesn't come from multiple partners (which in some cases has proven to be hazardous to your health), but from a nourishing and continued commitment to one person—a mate for life. Despite the continued commercialization of "the grass is greener" syndrome, men are realizing a committed, intimate relationship is much more fulfilling and satisfying. Extramarital affairs seem less appealing for a number of reasons—but no need to go into all of that. One would suspect you're reading this book to enrich your relationship with your wife, and not someone else. In *Shining Your Armour,* you'll find many practical suggestions to strengthen the love and devotion you had when you first took your marriage vows. As you read the suggestions in this book, be open to cultivate your own ideas. Your creativity will make a lasting impression on your wife.

Why
Be
Romantic
?

The cover of this book was intentionally stamped "For Married Men Only," and written for men who already have a commitment. I'll be direct and to the point—as a married man you have proposed to someone and said, "You and me, forever." You may have worded it differently, but it means the same thing. You decided you could make her life better if she would commit herself to you. She believed you then, and I intend to help you to convince her she should believe you now. My whole reason for writing this book is to help you to fulfill your original intentions when you asked your wife to marry you; that when she became committed to you, your lives would be made much better.

It doesn't take a Ph.D. in psychology to know women are different than men. In a nutshell, women respond to actions appealing to their emotions, such as sentimental cards and thoughtful gifts. Men, however, appreciate gestures that demonstrate respect. **One of the most important things to a woman is to know she is cherished and loved.** The objective of this book is to help you fill this need in your wife. Have you ever heard the lines "That's so romantic," or "He's so romantic," or worse yet, "Why aren't you more romantic!" You probably didn't even know what she was talking about—and that's my reason for writing this book. Men are being blamed for something that isn't taught in school, isn't talked about by the guys at work, nor mentioned in sports magazines. So don't feel guilty—just keep reading and learn.

This chapter asks the big question: **"Why Be Romantic?" The answer is very simple. Some women like it, the majority love it.** If you love your wife (you probably do or you wouldn't be reading this book), you want her to have the things she likes if there's any way you can give them to her. It goes back to the original reason of why you wanted to marry her. If you give her something she really wants, you've made her life a little better. Enough said. The real question then, is what exactly does she want? What is "being romantic," how do you measure it and how do you become "more romantic"? Good questions. I'll try to spell it out for you.

Romance is best defined as anything you do to demonstrate you care. In your case, it's anything you do for or to your wife to show her you love her. This may sound too easy, but notice the words "to show her." Romance gives the person you love something they can see, touch or feel as a symbol of your love. You may have let chances slip by to say or do something to express how special she is to you. The simple gesture of holding hands while you take a quiet walk, a meal with soft candlelight, or a little note saying "I Love You" convey so much and are treasured in her memory as an expression of your love. You might say to yourself, "She knows I love her." Yet, if you were arrested for loving your wife, would there be enough evidence to convict you? You're still married to her? Circumstantial. You give her your pay check every week? Not good enough. **What have you done recently, a little out of the ordinary, just to say "I love you"?**

Most women enjoy something that touches them emotionally. Little thoughtful reminders and actions creating an atmosphere of romance are what touches her heart. What appeals to her the most is your taking the time to express your love. When you were courting your wife, she knew you considered her someone special and you wanted to be with her. The same woman still loves to be courted, so don't forget it. Much has probably changed since your courtship. Your wife would welcome some assurance you're still together not out of convenience, habit, finances or children, but by choice. Such an assurance can only come from you, but its expression can be manifested by several romantic gestures. These tangible expressions and the newly-created memories will do just that for you.

The key to being romantic is expressing your love. One of the differences between men and women is that women like to be shown how much you love them in a variety of ways. Are you stumped for creative romantic ideas? Don't panic! That's what this book is all about. *Shining Your Armour* will suggest many different ways to express your love, but first you need to prepare your wife. Moving too fast may confuse her. Sudden changes in attitude or action could either throw her into shock or at least make her suspicious. You must also be careful not to do too much, too often or too soon. You'll have many opportunities to enhance the romance in your marriage. Flooding her with too much in a short period of time could lessen the impact of individual acts of kindness. So be patient and plan your romantic interludes. Read the next chapter carefully before doing anything drastic.

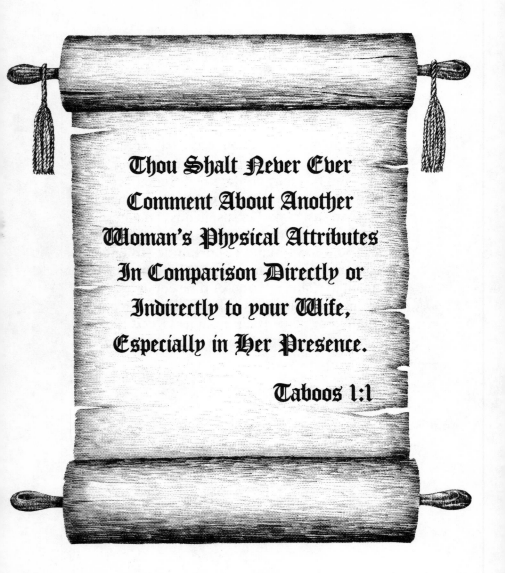

Thou Shalt Never Ever Comment About Another Woman's Physical Attributes In Comparison Directly or Indirectly to your Wife, Especially in Her Presence.

Taboos 1:1

Creative Romancing Commentary: Staring or drooling will cause the same effect on your wife as a comment, so avoid this as well.

Uhh...honey...what I meant to
say about her was.........

Romantic Attitudes

In this chapter, we will lay the groundwork for your wife's receptivity to your most romantic intentions. If she goes into shock, becomes very suspicious or asks questions like: "What did you do now?" or "What do you want to talk me into?" or just "What do you want?" then we've missed the mark. **The last thing you want is to give the impresson you have an ulterior motive or want something in return.** This will do more to destroy your romantic act and possibly more. Be patient; your rewards will be more than you thought possible. Your actions will lead to a marriage like the courtship you so enjoyed when your thoughts were of pleasing her, and hers of pleasing you. This is no fairy tale. You had romance and excitement then, and you can have it now.

One of the best ways to prepare your wife for more romance is to spend time with her alone. Tell her not only how much you love her but how you haven't shown her the depth of this love.

Your wife will appreciate your tenderness. It will also prepare her for some of the other suggestions in the following chapters.

One of the most important character traits in a relationship is humility. The real measure of a man is his ability to admit his weaknesses. You shouldn't feel condemned by these weaknesses, but you must recognize and acknowledge them. If problems plague your marriage, the worst thing you could do is to act or imply it must be her fault. This is an attitude problem—your attitude.

Let's go back to the original plan: "I married her because I loved her and thought our lives would be better if spent together." The greatest attitude you can have is to convince her you still feel the same way. What better way to say "I love you" than to try and change some things about your life to make hers better?

With humility on your side, using the rest of the suggestions in this book will be easy. I never met a man so stubborn he couldn't admit he fell a little short in his relationships. At this point, think of things you may have done or didn't do that aggravated your wife in some way. Don't try to figure out how to correct them just yet, but make note of them. You may not have to change those actions, merely change your attitude toward your wife and her reaction to them.

For example, you love to go hunting, fishing or golfing, and your wife has no interest in any of these activities. Show her you're not being selfish by agreeing that every time you spend a day away from her doing something only you enjoy, you'll then do something she enjoys—like going out to dinner, just the two of you, at her choice of restaurants. This

may seem like negotiating a business deal, but it
works. Just keep your attitude intact and you'll
enjoy two things: your favorite activity and the
pleasure of a woman who had looked forward to
your company. You may even find she's disap-
pointed if you cancel one of your activities from
time to time. If you want to get bonus points from
your wife, cancel your own plans but keep your
wife's plans anyway.

What's another way to show how much you care
about the every day occurrences in your wife's life?
Make sure you pay close attention to the occasional
aches and pains that accompany daily living. When
you notice even a scratch on your wife—acknowledge it, ask her how it happened and draw her
close. A gentle and tender touch will go along way in
broadcasting your concern. This goes for a sore
muscles from working around the house or at the
office. A spontaneous massage will reveal your
loving concern for her welfare. **Many times the most
romantic gesture is your response to her needs the
moment you recognize them.**

**Never allow your wife to believe or even suspect
she's taken for granted—not that you do or ever did.**
Performing the routine or daily duties of life can
leave your wife thinking you don't appreciate what
she does. It doesn't matter how much discussion
went into deciding who should do what duty; the
tasks are only bearable under the memory of your
latest show of appreciation. How often you demonstrate this appreciation, whether it be caring for the
kids or working a full-time job, is as important as
the most romantic evening you can devise. Showing
appreciation, on the other hand, can be accom-

plished in many ways, which we'll cover in upcoming chapters.

This statement might be hard to swallow, but it's as true as truth can be: **when it comes to being romantic, the little things count the most.** A combination of several smaller gestures can be far more meaningful and romantic than just one or two bigger events. Your thoughtfulness to give her pleasure means much more than you can imagine. Picking out a gift in her favorite color (even though it was difficult to find), a well-timed hug after she's had a hard day or just a gentle kiss on the cheek coupled with "I missed you today" are "little" things that mean a lot. And these "little" things will come to mind more and more as you start practicing the romantic tips in *Shining Your Armour*. Soon you'll be coming up with your own "little things" to thrill your wife. Now that you're undrstanding how to be romantic, let's get into some practical suggestions on showing the special woman in your life how much you love her.

Thou Shalt Never Give
your Wife Reason to
Believe or Even Suspect
you Have Taken Her for
Granted.

Taboos 1:2

Creative Romancing Commentary: Your wife's suspicion that you take her for granted will cause as much damage as actually doing so.

Whew! I've had a rough day!
The boss got on me for taking too many breaks, my
stapler broke and my computer screen keeps picking up glare.
So, what have you been doing all day?

The Written Word

This chapter introduces a very effective manner of communicating how you feel about your wife at different times. What are your thoughts when you're away from her? When you're near her? Or what comes to mind when her name is mentioned? These are perfect times to capture such thoughts and put them in writing for her benefit. Birthdays, anniversaries and other such occasions shouldn't be the only times to send cards or notes to your wife. When a card isn't expected, it'll impress your wife even more. **You'll find speaking in person or talking on the telephone doesn't have the lasting effect as something "penned on parchment."**

The time an thoughtfulness that you invest in creating a handwritten card will allow your wife to read it—and appreciate it—again and again. She can now hold in her hands a symbol of the depth of your feelings. They won't be mere words on a page to her, but a message explaining your innermost feelings, feelings you took the time and effort to write down. She will collect these are "little" treasures, cherish them through the years, and read them whenever she might occasionally wonder, "Does he still love me?"

Homemade cards should be in your own words and in your own handwriting. And don't worry about syntax—grammar or spelling will be the last thing on her mind. Ask your local printer or specialty stationery store about their selection of handmade parchment paper that can be folded in half and inserted in matching envelopes. Expressing you thoughts in different colored inks or calligraphy will undoubtedly give your wife more pleasure than any generic card.

EARLY MORNING WORDS OF LOVE

Soap Note

If you leave in the morning before your wife gets up, a great bulletin board for a casual "good morning" is the bathroom mirror. A bar of soap makes for a wonderful pen in this "love note in soap."

P.S. Be brief! Someone else might have to clean the mirror.

Surprise Out of the Fog

Before your wife takes a shower, take some anti-fogging liquid (usually found at a hardware store for your windshield) and write a note on the bathroom mirror. She'll be pleasantly surprised and curious of how you managed to write her a note without being there. You might find she won't erase it for a while. If so, this could be a good indicator that more surprises are welcome.

Shower Note

Another morning (or evening) surprise is a note hanging from the shower nozzle. A string or some tape on a sheet of paper will allow you to hang a creative greeting, like "Last time I was here, I was thinking about you," or "Here's looking at you, " or "What a beautiful bod!"

P.S. If she happens to turn on the water before seeing your note, using a permanent marker will help.

Hang-It-Up

A surprise love note in an unexpected place is another way to warm the heart to romance. A message can be hidden in your closet taped to a hanger. When your wife heads to the closet to change clothes, she'll be sure to notice your pleasant surprise. A suggestion for something to say is "Clothes can never hide the beauty of the woman I married."

Roll-a-Note

Another place for an early morning note would be hidden in a roll of toilet paper. This note not only has the element of surprise, but will probably provide a chuckle or two. Once again, be creative in what you say. Anything from "thinking of you" to an invitation to lunch would be appropriate.

P.S. If you have trouble writing on your brand of toilet paper with a ballpoint pen, then write the note on regular paper and roll it into the first few squares of toilet paper.

So You Need Coffee First Thing?

If your wife gets up in the morning and fixes breakfast for you and your kids, then an appropriately placed "thank you" note could change the way you're awakened that morning. She should be thanked for her care and consideration, don't you agree? If not, then go back and reread Chapter Two on "Romantic Attitudes." This note will prove not only that you notice what she does for you, but your appreciation it as well.

MIDDAY MESSAGES FROM THE HEART

Coupon Anyone?

Homemade coupons can be sent by mail to your wife for any of the activities you enjoy together. These coupons can be made from the parchment paper left over from your early morning notes. Just follow the examples on the next pages for ideas on how to design your own. Here's some suggestions of what you can give with a coupon: a dinner 'out;' a picnic; you'll do the laundry, dishes or cleaning; a backrub, foot massages or body massage; etc. Once again, these are just some of the things you can do. You know your wife, so think of some things she would enjoy.

Something Sweet?

This coupon could be for anything sweet, such as an ice cream cone in her favorite flavor and an escorted walk around a nearby park. The escort, of course, will be you. You may want to substitute ice cream for frozen yogurt or other sweets, such as a trip to a local chocolate shop. Make sure the coupon reads "redeemable upon receipt by her personal escort (that's you.) Satisfaction is guaranteed."

Massages

These coupons will be for different parts of her body massaged by head masseur (your name) in the elite massage parlor at (your address). Make several different coupons (such as one right foot massage, one left shoulder massage, a neck massage, etc.) redeemable immediately. If you don't know how to give a massage, pick up a book at a local bookstore. Even if you have to read the book out loud while doing the massage, she'll appreciate the effort. Who knows, she may decide to return the gesture...

A Manicure

This is a chance to allow your wife to be pampered a bit. Most women consider a manicure a luxury and rarely if ever receive one. If your wife falls into this category, she would probably enjoy such an offer. Directions on the coupon could instruct her to give the coupon to her private chauffeur (your name) to be driven to the salon of her choice for the manicure. Leave the date and time spaces blank so she can select a day most appropiate to her schedule, and you do the rest. As a bonus, note that a special free gift will be awarded to the recipient of this coupon after the manicure. While she's "redeeming her coupon," you could be buying a bracelet, a watch or perhaps a new ring to show off her new manicure.

A Bubble Bath?

What could be more relaxing to than a hot bubble bath after a long day? Many stores carry different oils and perfumed soaps for bathing. Knowing your wife's schedule, send her the coupon stating the time her free bubble bath will be ready for her enjoyment, and the address for the coupon's redemption (your home or perhaps a swanky hotel room rented for the night). Don't forget to indicate that the maitre d' (your name) will be on hand to cater to any other needs she might have. This is a good idea to use when you know she's having or going to have an especially rough day. By sending this coupon with a bouquet of fresh flowers, you'll lift her spirits for the rest of the day and allow her to anticipate an enchanted evening.

Love Note for Lunch

When you set up a lunch date with your wife, arrive early so you can be seated and inform your waiter or waitress you have a card you would like delivered. After she arrives, place your orders and excuse yourself to go to the men's room, the car, etc. When you leave, the waiter or waitress should deliver your handwritten card. While you're conspicuously absent from the table, she can read the note and decide how she'd like to respond.

It's very important to give her the time to appreciate your thoughtfulness. Sometimes an immediate reaction—perhaps one of shock or suspicion—isn't what the sender or recipient expects, as discussed in previous chapters. Give her time to think and respond, for both of your sakes.

Fill in the Blank?

Reminiscent of grade school crushes, this note is sent to your wife to remind her your love is still as fresh and innocent as a second grader—but with a more mature appreciation, of course. You can word the card to invite her to anything you desire, but add a certain childish flair.

I love you. Do you love me? Check box:
☐ yes   ☐ no   ☐ maybe

Will you run away with me this weekend?
Check box:
☐ yes   ☐ no   ☐ maybe

NOTES AT NIGHT

Your wife may need a combination of romantic gestures during an evening to overcome the pressures of her day.

Parking Ticket?

It might appear to be a parking ticket at first, but a simple note letting your wife know you were thinking of her will make the drive home much more pleasant. This can only be accomplished if you can get to her car without being seen. Once again, when you perform any romantic act, try not to be there so she can relish the gesture and the time and effort it took to perform it.

Welcome Home

At some party supply stores, you can order banners large enough to cover your front doorway. Like a soldier returning from war, you can greet your wife when she comes home from work or daily errands. Nothing will set the mood more than a large banner saying "Welcome Home (her name), I(We) Love You!"

Paycheck Dedication

You may let your wife take care of the finances, or at least deposit your paycheck. Yet earning a living is another manner of showing your devotion to your wife and family. This is how you feel, but it's probably another of the forgotten or unspoken principles of marriage. Next time you get paid, have a card ready to express your emotions:

> **I'm giving my best to meet our family's needs and hopefully provide some of life's extras. This paycheck symbolizes my work toward these goals. I present this to you as a token of my love for you (and our family).**

You can reword this to express your individual feelings. A paycheck dedication is your gift to your wife (or family), and once she's reminded of your dedication, she'll show her appreciation.

Pillow Talk

If your wife usually folds down the sheet before you go to bed at night, a nice note attached to her pillow reading, "Did I remember to tell you how much I love you today?" would be a pleasant surprise. This gentle question will answer itself as she ponders the man who wrote her this note. Again, try to be absent when she discovers this latest reminder. Give her time to decide how to respond to this treasured little "love note." Keep in mind she responds to a combination of little things creating a romantic atmosphere, so this could be a pleasant ending to a string of thoughtful gestures you may have done during that day.

Report Card

If you have children you understand how grades on a report card can impact one's self esteem. A good way to express your feelings about your wife's ability as a wife, mother, lover, friend, etc. is to give her a report card. A good place to leave this card could be the refrigerator with the grades in plain view for all to see. If you have a friend in the school system, you might even pick up a copy of the real thing.

Note: Make sure she gets nothing less than an A+ in any area.

Thou Shalt Never Make
Negative Comparative
Remarks About your
Wife and Some Other
Woman, Whether
Mother or Sister, and
Especially a former
Girlfriend.

Taboos 1:3

Creative Romancing Commentary: Statements of this type have scarred many a relationship permanently. Any denial or reversal of said statement is then suspected of being a lie.

Gosh.... this sure isn't the way
I've always had it before.

Romantic Gestures

Romantic gestures are actions showing your wife how much you love her. This is the manner in which you talk to her, the very words you say, what you do for her, what you don't do for her. As emphasized in the previous chapters, you must **show** your love. I'm assuming you love your wife and want to make her happy, or you wouldn't have read this far. Once you have the proper attitude on caring for your wife, these other suggestions will come easily.

All gestures are a product of love and consideration for your wife. Maybe before now you didn't quite know how to express these feelings in a way she would understand. Most men have difficulty sharing their deepest feelings with their wives. **Your wife needs to be reassured how much you care and quite often.** If you follow the suggestions in this book, you'll find it easier than you thought possible to emphasize your feelings. In return, she'll instinctively respond to your affections.

Romantic gestures are often connected with some of the suggestions found in the previous chapter, "The Written Word," because they aren't easily separated. Remember, it takes several combined "little" things to create a romantic atmosphere.

The upcoming pages offer a variety of suggestions to express yourself. Keep in mind three major points while reviewing these suggestions:

- **Because we are all individuals not all suggestions will fit your relationship.**

- **Use only the suggestions that appeal to you and would be appropiate for your wife.**

- **The suggested "written words" should be your own—expressions you've created and are comfortable with.**

The next section is broken into three time frames: morning, midday and night. This is to help you select the best actions for different times of the day.

Love Trails

As you perform these romantic gestures, you'll be creating a memory for your wife. Starting a scrapbook entitled "Love Trails" provides a perfect "home" for these memories. Use your first well-planned romantic gesture, complete with pictures of before and after (if possible) and put in the album. Suggest placing already-written notes in the album for "safe keeping." You will have created a memory book of the love you have aptly demonstrated. As you add more "love notes," photos and reminders of memorable occasions, she'll enjoy looking through the album again and again. This could very well become one of her most prized possessions. Wedding pictures may sit on the shelf and be looked at once a year at anniversary time, but this history of love in action will be treasured every time she makes another entry—which may be quite often once you see how she responds to your romantic gestures.

DAYBREAK DELIGHTS

Have a Wonderful Day . . .

On your way home from work, stop by a department store or a gift shop and pick up a tiny vase and a silk flower (or flowers). Keep this hidden, then leave it as a reminder of your sincere wish the next morning. On a small piece of paper, dedicate the flower(s) to wishing her a "wonderful day." Place the note and the vase on a counter, in the bathroom or somewhere she's sure to find it soon after you leave. You'll probably make her day, and she'll have a permanent reminder of your love.

Candlelight Breakfast

Instead of dinner, have breakfast by candlelight watching the sunrise— complete with toast, omelets, etc. Just check the daily newspaper for the approximate time of daybreak. If this is much earlier than you usually wake up, try to get to bed earlier the night before, telling your wife you have something special planned early the next morning. Always make sure the night before you have all the proper groceries and utensils for your early morning adventure. Most men can handle cooking a breakfast menu for their wife. Let her stay in bed until you're ready, which will also build her anticipation. Have the table set with your finest wares and the meal nearly prepared before you call your wife to dine. A flower basket centerpiece or a card prepared the day before will add the finishing touches to this romantic occasion. Plan this adventure for mornings when neither of you have to be anywhere else too early in case this gift of love leads to other activities.

High In The Sky Just You and I

Find a place offering hot air balloon rides. Hot air balloons usually leave at daybreak, so you will see one of nature's most beautiful sights—the dawning of a new day from the air. Most hot air balloon companies provide a brunch after landing as part of the package. Gliding high above the earth against the rising sun gives you the perfect backdrop for words of appreciation to the one who makes your "world go round."

Wake-Up Call

A romantic gesture need not be flamboyant in scope to portray a loving heart. A gentle kiss to wake your wife in the morning may suffice in place of a mountain of romantic words. If this is not your normal habit, it will mean even more to her.

LOVE'S DAYTIME DISTRACTIONS

Basket of Balloons

Send a "bouquet" of balloons tied to a small wicker basket resembling a hot air balloon. Put a combination of her favorite candies in the basket. This will fit nicely on her desk. As people walk by to inquire of the sender, she might share some of the candy. The card could say a variety of "sweet nothings," but could also be the perfect forerunner for a hot air balloon ride by saying, "Come fly away with me" or something similar.

"Happy Wednesday" Bouquet

If your wife works, then she's probably familiar with the Wednesday slump. You're halfway through the week but a long way from the weekend. This also could be sent to any at-home spouse—a homemaker has Wednesday slumps, too. A great pick-me-up is the "Happy Wednesday" bouquet of fresh flowers sent to her at her home or office on Wednesday morning. The card need only say "Happy Wednesday, Love (your name)." This may not shorten the work week, but it may occupy her mind with romantic thoughts of her generous husband.

I Love You

You are invited to a
Day Break
Delight!
For details
see your loving
husband.

Animal Love

Another way to deliver a memorable message is to couple it with a stuffed animal. Pick a small animal bringing to mind a special or appropiate message. For example: a tiger inspires "You bring out the tiger in me" or a bear "You can count on a bear hug from me." Be creative as you browse through shops carrying these romantic jewels. If you see more than one you can use, buy it now so you can surprise her later.

Love Grows...

Buy a flowering plant to create another special occasion. If she likes plants—or even if she doesn't—a message similar to "Like this plant my love for you is growing, and like this flower it continues to bloom," you're sure to elicit an emotional response. Every time the flowers bloom, your wife will remember your loving gesture.

No Time for Chores Galore

Many wives who have entered the work force are still trying to maintain high household standards. Many can't seem to find the extra time needed for such endeavors. Out of your love and appreciation for your wife's devotion, make a list of the things she plans to do as soon as she can find the time. When she's not around, call a cleaning service and get an estimate to complete the list's items; then schedule an appointment for all the chores to be finished in one day. Meanwhile, send an invitation to your wife to take her somewhere special (in case the cleaning service runs late) while the service completes the list. Instruct the service to leave an envelope you have prepared in advance on the front door. In this "note of love," tell her how you sincerely appreciate all she's done for you and how you treasure the time you have together.

This is Love Calling...

Make it a point to call your wife in the middle of the day just to say, "I was thinking of you, and I just wanted to call and say I love you." This may seem overly simple, but will multipy romantic thoughts on her part.

P.S. When you make this call, don't ask about anything else or you'll destroy the romantic gesture. She may then wonder why you really called, or if something else was on your mind.

Say "I Love You" in a Song

Select a love song you and your wife can identify with in your relationship and begin to think of a response or memory triggered by the lyrics of the song. This will be your own personal song dedication easily taped on the interlude of the song. From a local recording studio or with someone knowledgeable in audio, you can successfully dub your voice in at the proper time between verses or at any time when the song has an interlude. Picking a song such as Kenny Roger's "Lady" would bring to mind such statements as, "You're the only lady I'd ever want and I love you," or "Let me be your knight in shining armour, because I love you."

When you've made the cassette, pick the proper time to deliver it at work (or at home if she works at home) with a large bouquet of flowers with no card, only the cassette. Or you could take the paper cover out of the cassette case and make a new cover stating, "This cassette contains a message of love reserved only for you." Make sure you disguise your handwriting or get someone else to write it.

The suspense of who sent the bouquet may intrigue not only her, but everyone around her. You can imagine everyone going to the parking lot on the first available break to put the tape in the first tape deck they can find.

Just make sure the bouquet gets delivered to the right person. It could be embarrassing for the wrong woman to listen to your tape. The tape will then become a permanent reminder of your love, to be played anytime she wants to hear your loving voice.

All I Need is You . . .

Hire a chauffered limousine and drive to your wife's place of business around quitting time. The more people there, the better. Have the driver in full attire deliver a bouquet of romantic long-stemmed red roses with a card and a motel room key. The card should simply say, "The limousine is waiting, the room is rented, all I need is you. . ." You could sign the card or wait to capture her expression as she sees you leaning against the limousine, "dressed to kill." It might be a good idea to let a co-worker know what you're planning so as to prevent any delays of her getting off work. Have someone take pictures of her shocked expression as she receives the flowers and sees you for the first time.

The "limo" is waiting. The Champagne is chilled. All I need is you!

Queen for a Day?

For a very special occasion, like an important anniversary, you may want to go for this unique romantic gesture. This is not for the timid or the budget-minded—but it will never be forgotten by anyone who receives or observes this gesture of love.

For a reasonable donation to the high school music fund, you can hire a high school marching band to play a few songs in honor of your wife. Have an accomplice bring her outside to witness the performance in her honor. As she comes out, have your accomplice read a declaration from a large scroll, announcing, "(your wife) is declared Queen on (the date), over the kingdom of (your neighborhood), from this day forward. The captain of the guard, Sir (your name), is awaiting your every whim in defense of your crown and castle at (your address)." At that time, she's handed the scroll and crowned, then draped in royal robes about her shoulders. While the declaration is being read, have the trumpets sounding. After the coronation, have the band break into merry music until from behind the crowd, you ride up—mounted on a fine stallion, dressed as a knight in shining armour. All is silent when you dismount and approach your queen and kneel before her as you pledge your allegiance to her with your life. Then let the music play on as you take your queen to the castle. You can let the secret out so people will snap pictures or even have it recorded on video cassette for future memories.

ROMANTIC GESTURES AFTER WORK

Banner of Love

There are times you should proudly and publicly display your affections so your wife will know you're not ashamed of loving her totally and without reservation. One way to do this is to have a banner stretching over the front of your house from one end to the other. The banner should have tall letters for all to see with words like "Thanks for (however many) years of happiness! May I have (however many) more?" This will tell the world, as well as your wife, you're elated to be her husband and not ashamed to tell everyone.

P.S. If you have children, these romantic gestures shouldn't be hidden from them. Nothing will create a more secure environment for your children than to know their father loves their mother. You may find they'll be just as excited about it as she is. Besides you can always use a few accomplices.

Video for Two

To create a romantic mood some night, rent a few videos, or at least one with a romantic theme or plot. If you have a hard time finding one, just ask any female salesperson at your local video store. She'll probably know several. "Somewhere in Time," or "Romeo and Juliet" or the old standby "Gone with the Wind" are classic romantic movies. Of course, plan to enjoy this entertainment alone with your wife. The movie will create a romantic atmosphere, so flow with it. Keep in mind you're already home—so break out some pillows and get cozy as you watch this mood-setter together.

P.S. Don't forget the popcorn.

Canoe for Two

With the hustle and bustle of everyday living, you and your wife need time to yourselves. Break away from the normal environment to relax and talk to each other or maybe just enjoy each other's company. One of the best ways to accomplish this is to rent a canoe at a local park and leisurely paddle away the afternoon, talking about whatever comes to mind. Avoid discussions that might cause stress. Try to concentrate on pleasant topics, your appreciation of her dedication to you or the goals you may have set together.

Bubble Bath for Me?

In "The Written Word" section, there was a suggestion for a bubble bath coupon. On this occasion, give your wife no warning—just a pleasant gift to set the mood for the evening. Sometimes the element of surprise adds much more to setting a romantic mood.

Now there's more to it than just filling the tub with water and sprinkling in Mr. Bubble. Because no one appreciates a cold bubble bath, timing is important. Coordinate her arrival with the hot water supply. Go to a local bath store, pick up some fragrant bath soaps, oils, and candles for soft lighting. Select some relaxing, mellow mood music. To finish out the romantic atmosphere, fix her favorite beverage and serve her tubside. Be careful! You could end up in the tub, too. . .

Gazing into the Fire

If you have a fireplace, you already know the benefits of fireside chats with someone you love. But if you don't have a fireplace, try this alternative: find a nearby campground or area where you can set up a campfire. With this idea in mind,
you can either make a "camp date" or pretend you're in your living room cuddling on your favorite couch, gazing into the fire. Long-burning logs can be purchased from almost any hardware or grocery store. After a proper invitation (see Chapter Three), put the logs in your trunk, drinks in an ice chest and some marshmallows if you prefer, and chauffeur your wife to a night out in the wild gazing into a fire. This can be spontaneous or planned according to the weather. If you think your wife might be so inclined, take a tent and two sleeping bags; preferably ones that can be zipped together. This could turn into an all-night stargazing affair.

Moon Toast

Check calendars and weather reports for the perfect night to invite your wife on a "toast to the moon" walk around the neighborhood or a local park. Just bring two long-stemmed glasses and your favorite beverage. As you walk beneath the moonlight, stop and toast the moon for helping you see the extraordinary beauty of your companion. These little walks are perfect times to share thanks and appreciative thoughts with your wife or discover her desires for the future. The more you take these walks, the more comfortable and enjoyable they'll become to you and your wife. The soft lighting of a full moon will enhance the romantic atmosphere.

Official First Kiss Day

When you don't have an occasion to take your wife out, she'll appreciate it if you make one up. Say for example, "On this day (however many) years ago, we experienced our first kiss. In honor of Official First Kiss Day, I invite you to celebrate this memorable moment." Select an atmosphere or event conducive to a celebration of kissing. Don't worry if you can't get the day right. She'll be sure to celebrate anyway. An appropriate invitation to this celebration would be a helium balloon of big red lips attached to an oversized Hershey's chocolate Kiss. This is probably one event she won't pass on, so prepare your pucker.

Dinner Under the Stars

This dinner for two is enhanced by the starlight of a billion stars, adding sparkle to your evening meal. First arrange to pick up your wife and take her to your surprise dinner location. The location should be one free from all routines of everyday living. Try and to find someplace private, preferably with a gorgeous view. In the city, you could drive to the top of a deserted parking lot looking down over city lights as you watch the stars begin to shine. From your trunk, remove all the amenities for a dinner for two: a portable table with tablecloth, place settings for two, candles, a rose in a bud vase and a completely prepared menu ready for serving. Don't forget to put in your favorite tape of romantic music as you enjoy your meal under the majesty of the stars. Always be on the lookout for more great places to take your wife on such occasions.

Back to the '50s Night

Like the Ronnie Milsap song, take a trip back to the era of the '50s when the "golden arches" were young and Dairy Queen was the hangout till you went parking at your favorite "Lover's Lane." As always with a unique afternoon or evening, send an appropriate invitation to work or home. This will create atmosphere and anticipation, and she will wonder what you have planned. Tell her you plan a trip back in time, so dress accordingly. (You may make suggestions on what articles of clothing to wear.) One of the keys to this evening is to find a fitting "cruising" car from that era such as a '57 Thunderbird or a convertible 'Vette. Play a tape of Wolfman Jack's live radio broadcasts to send you both back in time. Take your date to McDonald's for hamburgers and Dairy Queen for a malt or to a '50s style diner—then "cruise" for awhile before you head to "Lover's Lane."

Dinner on Top of a Concrete Mountain

Sometimes you can arrange with a high rise's management to borrow its roof or a penthouse suite for a special occasion. This will provide a breathtaking view you haven't experienced before. Hire a catering service or accommmplice to prepare and serve your meal, further enhancing the atmosphere of a romantic *pas de deux*. The meal should be complete with full courses from appetizers to dessert, as well as a beautifully arranged table of the finest wares. Music can be provided by hired musicians performing your favorite love songs. After dinner, you may want to slow dance in the moonlight. Such royal treatment is the perfect backdrop for confessions of love and devotion for the years to come. You can also arrange for photographs of the two of you and the sights as you enjoy your special evening.

Nature's Hotel

Your wife may not like spending an entire vacation camping outdoors, but she's sure to like this little retreat. During the pleasant weather months, prearrange to have a tent and sleeping bags set up in a secluded spot overlooking a lake or stream with an excellent view for stargazing or moon-watching. There's nothing like the light of a full moon glistening over gently moving water. Logs can be provided to have the added benefit of a fire dancing in the night. Have a prepared meal in a basket to take along, as you spend a night at nature's hotel.

Tie a Little Ribbon. . .

Send a bouquet of flowers to your wife with a card saying something similiar to:

In appreciation of your love and my love for you, I would like to present a very special gift. We both await you. Love (your name)."

When she arrives after a long day of growing curiosity and anticipation, another note should be on the door with directional signs guiding her to a note on the bedroom door. A sign above this note will say to read this card before entering. The card should read something like this:

What greater gift can I give you than all of my love and all that I am. Enter here for tonight's gift.

When she opens the door, be standing there in your most alluring pose dressed in what she has considered your sexiest apparel or your "birthday suit" and a ribbon tied around you with a bow. She'll get the message.

P.S. Don't forget to unplug the phone and make a "Do not disturb" sign for the front door.

Good Ol' Country Picnic

One never outgrows classic romantic events like picnics in the country—complete with fried chicken, potato salad and a red checkered tablecloth. Take anything and everything you could possibly want to make this like the country picnics you've always heard about. Find a place where you can rent horses, canoes or hike into nature's hiding places. Somersaulting in a grassy field or laying on your back seeing how many faces you can find in the clouds are just some of the carefree activities you can do on a secluded picnic for two.

Sail On. . .

Another choice for a picnic for two would include the scenery of the ocean or at least a large lake in a rented (or borrowed) sailboat. A beautiful view and an afternoon breeze can provide a romantic atmosphere as you captain your ship to faraway places with your captive bride. Sail to a deserted island or peninsula away from the crowd to enjoy the company of your wife.

Caution: If your sailing ability would convince your wife arriving at the desired destination would nothing short of a miracle, then you might want to try another type of boat for your picnic.

Fur You and Fur Me

When cold weather outdoors just won't accommodate a picnic, try this alternative to still enjoy a picnic for two. Buy (or borrow) a (synthetic) fur rug to place in front of your fireplace and invite your wife to a picnic for two. Place all the necessary picnic needs in your basket as if you weren't at home then turn out all the lights using just the light of the flickering fire. It shouldn't be difficult for her to sense the romantic atmosphere in this setting.

Adam and Eve?

If you lean to the extravagant and/or exotic, you'll love to try this version of a picnic for two. Locate an island that can be accessed only by helicopter or seaplane to have a remote setting for your picnic. The requirement for selection is that no one will be on this island, only you and your wife. The accommodations available on the island (some might have a cabin), might determine your length of stay. But in the very least, you'll have a memorable time on your little slice of paradise. As you enjoy the sights and sounds of your tropical paradise (remembering you're all alone on your little island), you may want to commemorate marriage like the first couple by donning similiar apparel (or should I say lack of).

Love Lottery

If your wife loves to win anything, this just might thrill her. Send a telegram to your wife that reads, "You have won first place in the Love Lottery, entitling you to an all-expenses paid weekend at (local or distant resort) with your charming escort (your name). Your many deposits of love will go unrewarded no longer. For more details or reservation information, contact Love Unlimited (your address and phone number)."

Although flowers of any kind would be warmly received on this occasion, send this invitation with a large bouquet of red roses befitting the passion to come.

Somewhere Else in Time

Dress in a Victorian-style outfit and present her with a matching Victorian-style dress to dine at an appropriately old-fashioned restaurant with Victorian architecture, style and menu. As you mimic the romantic customs of an era that catered to romance, take a horse-drawn carriage ride and spend the night at a Victorian-style bed-and-breakfast inn. After a wonderful night of romance, take the rest of the day for a shopping spree purchasing memorabilia or have a picnic in the country, complete with wicker basket and all the fixings common to the Victorian era.

In-Law Love

Sometimes the indirect can be the most direct way of saying thank you for being a wonderful wife. Send a bouquet of flowers and a card of thanks to your in-laws for having created a wonderful daughter. This gesture will probably be mentioned to your wife sooner or later, and you'll surely benefit from the appreciation you've shown to not only your in-laws but to your wife as well.

Not Blink, Wink

Your wife needs to be assured privately an in public that you find her desirable. When you're at a party or just in the company of a few friends try to catch her eye and wink. She may be confused at first. If she inquires, merely state you were just flirting with a very beautiful woman. Maybe no one else in the room will see your daring moves, but your wife is sure to appreciate your playful charm. Winking is not the only way to get the message across. Try holding hands, a soft touch or even a gentle kiss. Public displays of affection will boldly state you're glad you are married to your wife and you're not ashamed to show it.

Love in the Wind and Waves

If at all possible, make plans to enjoy one of nature's most picturesque backgrounds for a truly romantic evening: picture a setting sun spreading its colors across the western sky while beneath it the deep blue sea sends gentle breezes of salty fresh air. This abundance of God's creation has put many in awe and begun countless enchanted evenings. When the sun is setting over the ocean, be on a balcony watching the lights of the sky sparkle in your wife's eyes. Rent a room high off the deck to get a wide view of this beautiful scene. Make late dinner reservations after you've toasted "the evening show" from your balcony. After dinner, enjoy Act II by pulling off your shoes and taking a moonlit walk along the beach while letting the sound of the waves serenade you. This is one of nature's most truly romantic settings.

Rose

Flower lore says a single rose is for lovers and a red-colored rose represents passion. Laying a rose across her pillow before you retire for the evening will say enough.

P.S. If she's not familiar with flower lore, attach a note.

Thou Shalt Never
Criticize your Wife
in Anything She
Can Never Change.

Taboos 1:4

Creative Romancing Commentary: Your wife's suspicion that she doesn't please you will cause not only dissatisfaction in herself, but worry if someone else (without this defect) is drawing your attention or affection.

Choosing a Romantic Gift

Choosing a gift is sometimes difficult. A romantic gift should imply your heartfelt love, affection and gratitude. Such a gift should naturally require careful thought and consideration. Gifts can be given any time of the year for any number of occasions, but a romantic gift should be given on romantic holidays like St. Valentine's Day, a wedding anniversary or a day you will henceforth celebrate as a "romantic reminder" to your love. **When there's no traditional occasion, a surprise romantic gift will have extra special meaning as a celebrated reminder of your devotion.**

There are many things to consider in choosing the right romantic gift. First, let's define a romantic gift as opposed to any other type. **A romantic gift is one that in its presentation and use displays your love by its very nature, inspiring an emotional recognition of your love and devotion.** Items needed for the normal duties of life, such as appliances, household items, etc. are better presented at other times. A romantic gift should please the eye and touch the heart, instead of being revered for its practicality. A prime example is fresh flowers. Fresh flowers will last only a short time before they lose their beauty and their scent, but for ages they have been considered the perfect romantic gift. The allure of flowers not only pleases a woman with beauty and scent, but makes her feel special as well.

Not only is choosing the right sentimental gift important, but it's presentation is equally as important. A bouquet of flowers thrown to your wife as you come in the door from work is better than nothing—but only slightly. The packaging of a gift is important because it produces the first impression. A poorly wrapped package gives an impression of a hurried choice, even when that might not be the case. Also, the attitude of its presentation will add much meaning to the gift. **Carefully chosen words (whether spoken or written) at the time of presentation will set the proper mood for the gift's reception before it's seen.**

Enough can't be said of the importance of a gift's presentation. The presentation is vital to the reception and the importance the recipient places on the gift. If the gift is merely handed over at a very unromantic time or out of a sense of duty because it's a certain occasion, it loses its romanticism. If there is an occasion, then determine from the nature of the gift if it should be presented at the party or later. Sometimes very personal gifts will embarrass your wife if presented in front of a crowd. So choose the presentation's timing with care.

A perfect backdrop or setting would be one of the suggestions in "Romantic Gestures." What better way to present a romantic gift than in a very romantic setting created by the giver of the gift?

Another important little detail is to make sure the package is properly wrapped befitting the gift. You wouldn't want an expensive piece of jewelry wrapped in newspaper—so make sure your package's wrapping is appealing to the eye. Many large department stores offer gift wrapping for a nominal fee. **Remember, the attitude in which your gift is given, the timing, and it's wrapping all contribute to making the first impression—make it a good one.**

It would be difficult, at best, to suggest romantic occasion gifts for your wife because every woman has different likes, dislikes, tastes, color preferences, etc. Although I cannot suggest a great number of gifts to purchase, I can point you in the right direction. Many popular gifts have been so for years and are still suitable, with a new twist to become both unique and special to your wife. I will suggest a few variations of the "ol' standbys." Always be on the lookout for other gifts to either buy now for a presentation later, or make note to come back another time.

Flowers

Flowers may be naturally impractical and extravagant, but they're still considered by many as the most romantic gift a woman can receive. Still, very few lovers know the ancient lore behind flowers. Nearly every variety of flower conveys a special meaning or message. Daisies mean "I'm thinking about you"; peach blossoms stand for love and beauty; purple flowers tell the recipient you're her love slave or captive; and red roses mean passion. If you'd like to know more of the different legends, your local florist will be happy to assist in your selection.

You'll notice I suggest in many of the "Romantic Gestures" to send invitations with flowers. An arrangement of fresh flowers appeals to the eye, which always seem to set the mood for romance. When sending flowers as a gift, keep some key points in mind. Although long stem red roses are beautiful, they have almost become commonplace. Your wife will think you've put so much more time and thought into a gift if you have an arrangement made with a variety of different colored roses. To insure you did take the time to choose the colors, have a card say something about how the legend of those flowers or the colors relate to your relationship.

If you don't want to send a bouquet, sometimes a beautiful bud vase with a perfect single flower coupled with a carefully worded card will state your feelings just as well. If at all possible, have the flowers delivered to your wife where she can show off your loving gesture, such as her office if she works outside the home.

If price is a consideration, stop at a roadside flower mart. Some grocery chains have in-store florists with seasonal flowers at more reasonable prices. You can also find a wide variety of flowering plants to make attractive gifts, producing new joy each time the plant blooms, as stated earlier.

An alternative to fresh flowers are silk arrangements. These are best when sent with a gift you'll expect her to display or use as an attractive centerpiece. Make sure these are real silk or of comparative quality, since any gift should be of high quality, because it will reflect your attitude towards your wife.

Because
I Love You,
your
Husband

Chocolates?

Heart-shaped boxes of chocolates seem to magically appear on shelves everywhere near St. Valentine's Day. Lovers usually gobble up these boxes as last minute gifts by February 14. Chocolate is an appropriate romantic gift because, according to theory, an ingredient in chocolate called phenylethylamine supposedly imitates the hormonal effects of being in love. Chocolate can be presented in a variety of forms from cream-filled hearts to gift boxes of 24 carat gold-wrapped replicas of your face or hers. You can also send long-stemmed flowers made of white, milk or dark chocolate. A trip to a local chocolate store can provide endless ideas to satisfy your wife's sweet tooth.

The Sweet Scents of Love

Perfumes have been around for centuries and
have been considered prized possessions in the past.
One of the gifts of the Magi was expensive perfume.
Today, perfume is used to enhance the sensuality of
the wearer. Perfumes make perfect gifts because
they appeal to your wife's senses; however, there are
a few guidelines to keep in mind.

Choosing the right perfume from the wide selection at a department store's perfume counter is like
trying to shoot holes in the moon with a slingshot.
Since many of today's perfumes change scents as
they mix with one's own body chemistry, finding the
one that pleases either her or you could be a shot in
the dark. To choose perfume properly, either select
one she already uses or ask her (in the guise of
curiosity) about certain ones you thought she would
like. You might inquire from someone else what
type of perfume she's wearing if that particular scent
appeals to you, and run the name by your wife to see
if she has tried it before.

Jewelry

Jewelry is another very popular gift item, but is difficult to buy without knowledge of the recipient's personal taste. Since the variety of designs appeals to each persons' taste, you might find it difficult to select an item you know she would like. During one of your browsing walks through a shopping mall, ask about her favorite gemstones and settings, then make a note for future reference.

Find out if her favorite type of metal is brass, pewter, silver, gold, etc. You can judge the particular styles she might like by noticing her favorite pieces of jewelry. Millions of dollars have been spent on a single gift of jewelry in an expression of love. As with any gift, it matters more what the giver feels for the person than the cost of the gift. The gift is merely the expression of the gift-giver's feelings.

Some gifts can never compare to the devotion and sacrifice a person will give to the one he or she loves. A gift is usually a token of appreciation for the opportunity to be able to love someone. These thoughts can sometimes be conveyed in words, delivered with the gift to relay even more meaning.

Keep a Record . . .

The best way to prepare yourself for gift purchases is to have some kind of filing system to keep track of your wife's preferences. Keep space available for items you might want to buy in the future, or for occasions in the distant future. If you see such an item in a store, make sure it will be available when that occasion arrives. Write down which store, its location, hours and phone number. If you buy your wife certain clothing items, you'll need a current dress size, blouse size, shoe size, etc. It might help to know which stores your wife loves to frequent, so you can create a shopping spree with gift certificates.

Palate Pleasers

Sometimes a romantic gift is in the shape of a favorite food, such as a heart-shaped pizza served with wine on a candlelit table. There are many foods that can be fashioned into a heart shape for both of you to enjoy. Why not try breakfast in bed with heart-shaped waffles, a rose and passion fruit? Let your imagination run wild as she enjoys her favorite foods.

One of a Kind

Your wife is unique. Because there's no one like her in all the world, the gift you choose should reflect these sentiments. What better way to present this feeling than to have a gift made of the finest material and handcrafted to your specifications for her pleasure? As you learn her favorite types of metals, precious stones or other types of material she desires, you can choose the components of a special gift designed especially for her. Pick a theme for your gift to emphasize your deepest intimacies. A blue topaz set in a gold setting could say:

> **This gift reminds me of the first time
> I saw you. I gazed into the beautiful
> blue eyes against your golden skin,
> and I've been a captive to your love
> ever since.**

Picking a theme may take some thought and coordination to create the perfect gift to say "I love you." As you observe the craft of others skilled in making custom gifts of metals or precious gems let your imagination run wild. You may have something stored in your creative mind no one ever thought of as a gift. Let your creativity flow in this expression of love, and you'll be rewarded with a special gratitude you've never known before.

You'll Always Be. . .

After many years of marriage and several children, some women lose their girlish figure and dream of their youthful years when they danced and played. The following gift would say how much you care and love the woman you met, romanced and married. Find a craftsman skilled in the art of making crystal sculptures and have a ballerina carved to set on a pedestal with the carved inscription, "You'll always be my ballerina girl, Love (your name)." This could sit upon a music box playing the love song "Ballerina Girl."

This type of gift would only appeal to a few special women. But the idea is to portray your wife's uniqueness while making a fitting tribute of your love for her. Keep in mind other shapes and likenesses would be just as appealing if applicable, such as former athletes, beauty contestants, etc.

Medal of Honor

To honor your wife for her outstanding ability to care for you or your family, a fitting gesture would be to have a medal or trophy designed just for her. Choose any number of styles from a trophy store and make sure you present it with the spirit of the message it states. Have the trophy inscribed with the words closest to your heartfelt feelings. Trophies are made to be displayed so keep in mind she may want to proudly place it on a mantle or shelf to brag about her loving husband.

Gift of Love

Not every gift has to be expensive to be a special gift from the heart. Sometimes you may find yourself looking for a very special gift no craftman could quite create. You may want to express your devotion by using this suggestion as an example of the undying appreciation and love you have for your wife.

This gift should be at least three boxes specially wrapped starting with a larger box down to a smaller one. The wrapping of each could vary with the size from very nice wrappings on the larger to exquisite papers on the smaller boxes. The setting for this special gift should be the most romantic you can arrange. Present the gift when the two of you are alone. In the smallest box should be a beautiful message on handmade paper in the shape of a non-folding card or small scroll and sealed with decorative sealing wax. A professional calligrapher could pen your words with care and quality befitting the message. The words on this card should express your deepest sentiments:

"The gift I give to you cannot be contained in a box nor stored anywhere. It must be given or it will die, and if given it will grow. This gift takes many shapes and many forms. The greatest and most precious gift I can give, I give to you, my wife. My gift to you is my Love."

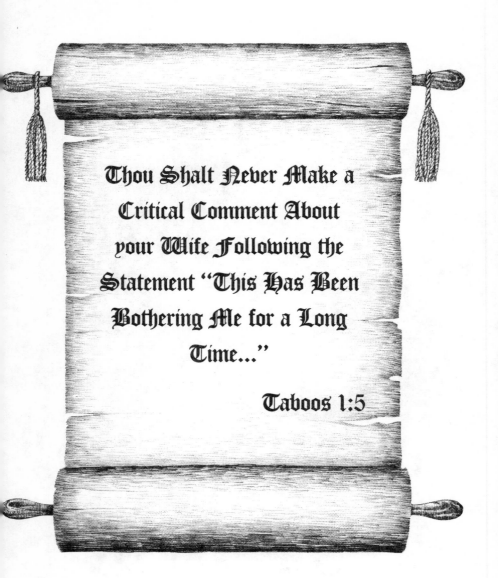

Thou Shalt Never Make a Critical Comment About your Wife Following the Statement "This Has Been Bothering Me for a Long Time..."

Taboos 1:5

Creative Romancing Commentary: Now that you finally told her this problem, your wife wonders what else is bothering you. Your disclosure will cause her undue stress and mistrust.

...And I've been meaning to tell you honey....
that outfit has really bothered me for a long time.

Preserving Romantic Memories

Many events in our lives are so pleasant we would love to relive them to feel the joy and emotion again. This is true of a romantic gesture where people were able to experience the joy of both expressing and receiving this love. These memories, which can bring about a smile in the lonely hours when you're apart from your loved one, should be preserved so they can be experienced and enjoyed over and over again. **If you're willing to spend the time and care to present your love to your wife, then be considerate enough to let her enjoy the expression more than once.**

A kind and thoughtful gesture can be preserved indefinately if you take the time now to secure the details in pictures, words, videos, etc. The previous pages suggested various invitations and different activities to create a romantic atmosphere, but this chapter will discuss how to keep the romantic gesture alive to be enjoyed over and over again.

The follow-up of a romantic gesture will be the gifts you present to your wife to remind her of the event. If you have nothing to remember the event by, then eventually the details you took so much time to prepare will fade in her memory.

Some of the reminders of an event you could give your wife are pictures of the two of you enjoying the activities, or a handwritten card thanking her for accepting your invitation and sharing a part of her life with you on that particular date. As most gifts are usually presented during a romantic setting, the gift is a reminder of the date; but if you add some reminders of the romantic setting in which you presented the gift, it will continue to carry that special meaning it had at the time of presentation.

Another suggestion to create a constant reminder of a romantic occasion is to deliver a bouquet of silk flowers with a double-framed picture of the two of you during the romantic event. Don't forget to include the thank you card. The picture could be on one side and the self-composed card on the other. In the wording, you could mention the occasion, the date or something you discussed that evening. This could be displayed as a conversation piece, so she may tell others what a wonderful evening you prepared for her. The silk flowers could be placed in a unique vase chosen because it reminds you of the place or the event. The flowers, being silk, will never fade or die so they provide an everlasting reminder.

A suggestion at the beginning of Chapter Four on "Romantic Gestures" was entitled "Love Trails." This was a good example of how to preserve a memory. Invitation cards as well as pictures are prime objects for this living legacy of love. It is sure to touch her heart each and every time she goes through the pages and sees your loving consideration—not only the first time, but that you cared enough to preserve the memory forever.

The Ultimate Evening

The following suggestion is extravagant, requiring much of coordination, planning and the use of all three phases of a truly romantic gesture. You'll clearly realize the significance of the invitation, the rendezvous/activity and the follow-up. You can be sure this event will be remembered for a long time.

This evening is designed for a very special occasion, such as a second honeymoon. Or you may desire to show your wife that no expense should be spared for a woman who means so much. This evening will be filled with many romantic gestures—a veritable night to remember. Such a night, for most women, is nothing more than a fantasy; but for your wife, it can be a reality to be relived over and over again each time she remembers the love expressed in this gesture. I'll go through the evening step-by-step, explaining in detail how each phase should be handled in advance.

Start the evening by delivering a special invitation with a large bouquet of fresh flowers. The invitation is a card with the front cover as an 8 x 10 photograph of you with an outstretched hand ready to escort her into the back of a limousine. The card contains a formal invitation, skillfully written to ask your wife to join you for a very special evening. If you know your wife's schedule, make sure she won't have any conflicting activities with the date you've chosen.

Upon accepting the invitation, your wife should receive very explicit instructions on what time the limousine will arrive. Suggest proper attire or present her with a box containing a complete evening ensemble (purchased by you at an earlier date). If necessary, arrangements should also be made for a babysitter. The limousine driver will knock on her door at precisely the time stated on the invitation. Of course, you're not there as you stated in the invitation, you will meet her later. If the date isn't the same day the invitation is sent, then plan to leave the house earlier that evening without divulging any information to the upcoming events. Change into your evening attire somewhere else.

As the driver escorts her to the limousine and seats her comfortably, he will then play a video prepared by you. This will be a composition of your thoughts and deepest sentiments, and how you'd like to express these feelings this evening. Dressed in different outfits with different backdrops, you describe a series of what you might have done. But, of course, you decided to do something else instead, which will be a surprise.

You inform her to be comfortable and patient as she enjoys the specially-selected love songs, and tastes the special gift of chocolates on the seat next to her. You mention you'll be with her shortly. The chocolates she finds are miniature sculptures of your face wrapped in gold foil. As she listens to the love songs playing in the background, she hears your voice in the musical interludes dedicating the songs to her as a token of love. Have the driver take her to the airport, and standing next to a chartered plane, there you are—dressed in a tuxedo, ready to enjoy a special evening together. After take-off, you fly west for a bird's eye view of the setting sun as you toast the evening show with your favorite beverage. As the stars start to twinkle and the moon begins to

shine, your pilot flies to the restaurant you have chosen. The staff of this famous five-star inn is awaiting your arrival and greets you and your wife by name. Your table has been prepared as requested. Reserving the table are laser engraved nameplates with her name on one and yours on the other. On her placemat is a card with a long-stemmed red rose and a special message composed by you. If you wife has green eyes, you could say something like this:

> **"A touch of green, the color of beautiful eyes**
>
> **A touch of red, the color of a beautiful smile**
>
> **Singularly and by itself it's just as beautiful**
>
> **It reminded me so much of you, I thought you should have one."**

As you dine on delicacies chosen from a menu with no prices to distract her choice, have someone photograph the two of you enjoying your meal by candlelight, capturing the moment forever. At this time, a specially-chosen gift can be presented to your wife. Perhaps after dinner a walk in the moonlight around a lake would be in order. To finish the evening, retire to the privacy of the honeymoon suite at the inn, complete with breakfast in the morning sent up on a dumb waiter or room service for breakfast in bed. A limousine should pick you up the next morning to drive you back to your residence.

To preserve the moment forever, deliver an exquisite "thank-you" note framed with an 8 x 10 photograph of the two of you at your table, along with a beautiful arrangement of silk flowers in a hand-painted (or etched) vase with the date and occasion of your **"Ultimate Evening."**

Thank you for a night I will always treasure!

Thou Shalt Never Make a Negative Comment About a New Hairstyle Tried by your Wife.

Taboos 1:6

Creative Romancing Commentary: This falls close to the category of something she cannot change, especially if her hair was cut. Keep in mind the change was an attempt to improve her appearance. Diplomatic conversations can help you express your preference in hairstyles only after the initial shock has passed.

May the
words of
these pages
lift your
marriage
to new
heights.

Gabriel

For information on other books by Gabriel H. Vaughn or to order additional copies of *Shining Your Armour* ($8.95 plus $2.50 postage and handling), write to:

Shining Your Armour, Inc.
1018 West Harvard Street
Orlando, FL 32804

About the Author

Gabriel H. Vaughn is an entrepreneur, author and speaker. His unique but very practical style and approach on current issues affecting relationships stems from his business experience and military service in the Air Force (1973-1977).

Prior to initiating his writing career several years ago, Vaughn developed and operated a successful business in addition to providing developmental research for several businesses and business ventures.

For his book *Shining Your Armour*, Vaughn spent over 3,000 hours in extensive research, and conducted an indepth study on "creative romancing" in conjunction with the University of Central Florida. In addition, he has also developed workshops on marital relationships as well as other topics.

Born, raised and educated in the southern United States, Vaughn now resides in Orlando, Florida. In addition to his writing, Vaughn is also a member of a national speakers bureau and travels extensively speaking to men on masculinity and chivalrous character.

Vaughn is currently writing *Knights of the 90s* which will outline the seven character traits of a man that would make him a knight in this decade. Also on Vaughn's agenda is a sequel to *Shining Your Armour*, which will be entitled *Shining Your Knight—For Women Only*.

NOTES

NOTES